Dream On Dreamers

A Book Of Inspiration

LLEWELLYN C. RADFORD II

DEDICATION

This book is dedicated to my mother and father. I want to thank my mother for never giving up on me and inspiring me to never quit. She taught me what it means to fight. I wish my father was here to see everything that's happening but I thank God that he was here for 21 years of my life. This book is also dedicated to all the dreamers out there, Dream On Dreamers!

CONTENTS

Acknowledgments

ACKNOWLEDGMENTS

I want to acknowledge my brother Llew for sticking by my side and letting me be a big brother as well as all of my younger siblings, I love y'all so much. Thank you. I want to acknowledge my friend and brother Blake Kelly, we continue to stick by each other as if we share the same blood... It's only the beginning brother. I have too many friends and family members to list, just know that I acknowledge you all because without your constant motivation and love I would have given up a long time ago. God has placed you all in my life for a reason and I am so appreciative. Last but not least, I want to acknowledge my helpmate, my teammate, and my partner in crime Sara Holland. You are so new to my life, yet you have made such huge affects on me already. You helped me complete this book, we're going to new heights together and I look forward to everything God has in store for us. Thank you! God bless you all!

LLEWELLYN C. RADFORD

Dreams of Being a Star

I want to be famous, Momma

I want to be a star

Yeah, I want my education

Yeah, I know it's going to be hard

But I want to be a star

It's a road that's congested, with no clear finish line

But I'm battle-tested, and I will see the finish line

See, I serve a God that knows no limits

A God that gives me no room for quitting

So I'm holding my ground

Chin high, my heart's big

And my mind hears its sound

I've got friends and family that truly believe

They have even put up their money for me to

succeed

3

Just the thought of their support sometimes is all I
need

When people ask how's it going in LA

I say, it ain't easy, but I'm still here babayyy!

See, I'm going to make it, fightin' tooth and nail

I'm on a train to success and it won't derail

I sleep and wake up like this can't be real

But everything happens for a reason and

THIS is GOD'S will!

When I dream I see space and constellations

I want to be a star

Ever since I realized that—no hesitations

I mean, I'm human

I have my reservations

But I quickly fix my thoughts

Because God already reserved my spot at the top

So all you dreamers out there

Who want more than usual

Who don't want to settle for the norm

The nine-to-five don't really work

It's not what you yearn

Not that with a nine-to-five you're doing anything

wrong

Your bank account is probably larger than mine

But I won't forever sing the I'm broke song

I can smell it I can taste it

It's almost my turn

Daily I live, fire lit and passionate

Nope, failure's not an option, I can't fathom it

So let's keep pushing till the cash comes in

Us dreamers we do this for those who can't, won't,

and just don't

So don't you quit, no you can't, no you won't

See, you dreamed that dream for a reason

That negativity is only here for a season

I'm going to be a star and I won't stop believing

DREAM ON, DREAMERS!

Breakdown

This piece is based on a conversation I had with my momma about going into entertainment. That was the initial conversation when I decided I no longer wanted to focus on my education and I wanted to be famous. I hadn't fallen in love with the craft of acting just yet, but I knew I wanted to be on the main stage, for lack of better words. My momma always preached about going to college, especially as a black man in our society. I knew that would better my chances of success, but I have a dream that I knew I could achieve somehow, some way. Although I stepped out on faith with my dreams, there was still work to be done. It didn't stop there. I've worked an array of jobs, from a hardworking business-to-business office supply salesman to construction. Faith without works is dead. Things don't always go as planned, but if you just keep believing and trusting in God, everything will be just fine.

Ima Stand Tall

I've got a passion for rapping and acting so

I guess my love for poetry is a preconceived notion

I'm hoping to be a motivational spokesman so I

guess modeling being one of my things is

something that you're now knowing

I thank God for my past, present, and future success

Slow progress is better than no progress but without

struggle there's no progress

I digress.

But before I drop this microphone and allow myself

to be left alone

Well . . . I'm really never alone

I always got my phone

And I feel six is wrong for me being in the zone

And just one for me touching home

I pray daily that he's blessing homes

I pray daily that he's blessing homes

See, I'm just that guy on the TV show in the
wheelchair

Even when I don't feel well I'm still there

I just wanna be successful but dream chasing gets
so stressful

No studying for what this test for

So what I do?

Take my dreams by the horns and stress more

The Bible says he'll never put more on me than I
can bear

But sometimes I feel the weight on my back can be
unfair

I'm well aware that's a human moment and he's
always there

9

Guess I'm ready for whatever if I slip and fall

Or it gets a little dark in the tunnel hall

Ima fight till the end; I want it all

In the midst of this battle

Ima stand tall

Dream On, Dreamers.

Breakdown

This was the first piece I ever wrote in LA. When I
moved to Los Angeles from Newport News,
Virginia, I really had no clue what was going to
happen. I was just trusting God. My faith in him and
my dream is what drove me. With that being said;
adversity, trials, and tribulations would definitely
occur. I had friends to talk to back on the East Coast
but I found writing to be my true therapy. It was
how I got by; I just wrote.

I remember sharing "Ima Stand Tall" with my brother and mother, knowing that this was another avenue for me. But what really let me know I had to share my writings with the world was when people I did—and didn't—know told me they were inspired. I love to inspire, and I knew that I had to get my message first to those from similar backgrounds—government and low-income housing, the hoods, the ghettos. The places that, for the most part, if you're not hustling, hooping, or playing football, you were pretty much destined for mediocrity in most eyes.

I had to let people know that although I was struggling, if you fight, you can really accomplish whatever it is you want. No dream is too big, no vision too wide. Nobody is perfect, but God is, and he didn't give us desires, gifts, and talents for nothing. I want you to know that God isn't going to give you gifts and talents and not provide a way to get there; but you have to trust him, and keep fighting.

It doesn't stop in the hood, though; there are people everywhere who need to be inspired, and they don't feel they can accomplish the "big dreams." I'm here to tell you that you can. The first step is believing that you can do it; everything starts in your mind. If you don't believe you can do it, how can you ever start to physically make anything happen? Then you can't stop just because things get a little challenging. It's all about how you view things and understand them; perspective versus perception. That's why I say NO MATTER WHAT IMA STAND TALL. How else do you expect to **see** your way through? Start and keep going. The only way you know you made it is if you don't stop.

When

When, I ask; to whom, I don't know

The answer seems so far to go

When the question arises

When I have the audacity to interrogate the on-time

God

Who provides us

Everything we need and more

I just sit back and cycle through my mind

Time after time after time

He pulled me out that mess

He relieved me of my stress

Even when I couldn't

He pulled out my best

See, this life is a journey

Better yet an obstacle course and

We're going to fall, trip, and stumble

But don't back down from the fight—be ready to

rumble

And don't just take heed from my mumbling words

Verse by verse

Think positive similes

Because if my memory serves me right

He's never done anything to hinder me

Some cannot see but I've been blessed to think

ahead of me

Thank God for blessing me intellectually

And that's the same reason there's no quit in me

But I'm human, feel me

My feelings sometimes kill me

My cojones ain't big enough to kill me

I'm still me.

Me is strong, but me is affected emotionally

By what I haven't been and what I'm hoping to be

What loved ones say is just poking me

Prolly 'cause they think it's just a joke to me

But this dream ain't a joke to me not a hoax to be

So how much poking before you're not able to

know it's me

Notice me!

I have so much for the world to see

When?

I just want a peak

I just want to see

I mean, I believe and I know it's coming

But I'm not going opposite so why isn't it running

to me

When?

When will it happen?

I'm waiting for the day I don't even contemplate trapping

When that type of traffic is obsolete from my mathematics

When what I'm adding can be subtracted from my family's magic

So when is like Raj asking, "What's happening?"

I don't know.

It's just happening.

So Ima let the happenings happen

Satisfaction is overrated

Hope and dreams are my fuel; Ima make it

When?

Who cares because Ima be just fine

Whenever when is

It'll be right on time

Dream On, Dreamers.

Breakdown

Everyone wants to know when! Whether you consider yourself a dreamer or not, most of us want to know when is that ultimate success that we fight tooth and nail for daily; when is it coming? As an artist it is tough not having a guaranteed check, not knowing if you will work the next week or the next day. But to proceed becomes second nature if you love what you do, like I do. *When* simply becomes a piece of the puzzle. You have to keep your vision forward; how else will you see where you're going? Every step of the way is *when* before it happened, so just keep going and it'll be right on time, like it always has been. God won't let us down.

Success Story in the Making

Nobody said it would be easy—shoot, nobody said much of anything

I just dove in, faith first

Now that I think about it, maybe somebody said something, and maybe I wasn't listening

But I wanted to do what I wanted so I just dove in, face first

My passion screamed so loud

Vocal opinions were surely drowned

I knew the journey wouldn't be swift

But I believed I could achieve quick

For I was blessed with a gift

But that's just it

These talents, these gifts…

They are a blessing from God

The success, not on my time, but when he sees fit

No specific sequence

That's reality served, deep dish

Tough roads behind and ahead

That'll make your mind—or literally your entire

being—coil like a fetus

Believing when everyone stops seeing

When you dreaming is seeming foolish

But no folly in a dream

For sleep without a dream is boring

For some just snoring

An inadequate touch outside the box

Normal, putting on socks in the cold

But what's normal? even matching socks has gotten

old

Bold fantasies drowning your mind like submarines

The impregnation of more than what they said was

for you

When the idea of waking up

Going to work

And coming home began to bore you

Blinded by my vision

I don't see it *not* working

That's the mentality of a success story in the

making

None of this is scripted

I continue on even when hurting

That's the mentality of a success story in the

making

I don't know, I can't take it

I mean, I'm human, but at the end I still say I'm

gonna make it

That's the mentality of a success story in the

making

DREAM ON, DREAMERS!

Breakdown

I wrote this understanding the journey I chose. I

chose entertainment because it was in my heart. I

realized just going to work and coming home

wasn't enough for me. I didn't know why at first; I

thought I just wanted to be famous. But then I

realized it was about more than me. I love to

inspire, and I was blessed with the equipment to do

so.

I am blessed with talents and gifts, and I

must share them with the world. But that doesn't

mean I'm going to skip, jump, and hop into success.

Everybody's route is different, and surely I'm

blessed—but it ain't easy. I still have faith. I still believe, and nobody can make me believe otherwise.

From what I've seen, being successful means continuing on no matter what. Nobody was ever successful by stopping. It all starts in the mind; you can't continue on if you don't believe you can. You have to have the mentality of a success story in the making en route to success. Sometimes no one will believe, and sometimes everyone will believe. Sometimes you won't want to continue on, and sometimes you'll feel you made it…but until you get there literally, we must keep going, and that's the mentality of a success story in the making.

Dusk to Dawn

As I attempt to guide my words with dawn's light

quickly approaching

I must say…I hate sleepless nights

I hate having so many thoughts that I can't fully

wrap my mind around the idea of sleeping

When I feel weeping would be more beneficial

But my eyes are as dry as a Las Vegas summer

Or your corners when you first awake in the

morning

I just want happiness and success

I don't wanna stress no more

My passion and thirst for a challenge finds me

unbalanced

Lord knows I hate stress

And where I'm trying to get

Plus Ima die one day

This life ain't timeless

Someone could've chimed in

Guess right now that's not my assignment

Pain . . . Struggle . . . Stress . . .

You reap what you sow

What I'm temporarily assigned with

How bold to express the truth

I think it's just real

Honesty to tell the truth

Sick and tired of biting my tongue and holding back

to spare others

No one cares for my feelings

I'm not a spared brother

But no.

See, our journeys are specific to us

That's why when I get all worked up

I sit down and open up

There's no rush

God has control

A human being I am

Since a baby by nature we fuss

When you want something bad it sucks

Because anything worth having we gotta work hard

for

Blood, sweat, and tears

We get scarred for

Puttin' in years

A career, not just a job

Becomes a part of you

Of your culture

The crazy thing is

I'm only getting closer

Closer to all I've hoped for and more

I've spoken things into existence

So I won't be surprised when I get it

But it's not just I

It's about more than me

Souls to Christ

Negative to positive

Dreams to reality

That's actuality

Love is coming

Just be patient

Loneliness is leaving

Just be patient

I WANT IT NOW!

I can't take it

God is right here with me

I will make it

DREAM ON, DREAMERS!

Breakdown

Writing this was how I was feeling at the moment. I couldn't sleep, and success was on my mind. The process is what I've learned to enjoy. On the way to success there will be bumps and bruises, but you have to fight on. I've realized there's more to life than just me. My talents and gifts were meant to assist in furthering God's kingdom. When you realize it's not just about you, the process is easier to understand, and you will be able to move forward—even in the tough times—just a little bit better. We all want it right now, but right now might not be right for the moment. The right now is whenever it's supposed to be and it will be right on time…just trust God and keep moving.

IDK

I don't know what to write

I don't know what to say

I don't know so I'm writing what I'm thinking

Exactly the thoughts while simultaneously blinking

Hoping that this paper comes alive with the

assistance of the ink

In this Bic Round Stic

The passion and aspirations drive me

Wildly living while opposing timid thoughts

Pushing myself when some would probably stop

Some would probably just return to the old block

Return to the old block like a lost letter

I won't quit—never

Not till it's better

Better than ever!

My better may not be yours

My best is better than my words

I compile sentences to not just inspire myself

They're engineered selflessly to ignite the burning

in others

Dreaming is healthy

Action is necessary

Hope and faith are the bridge in between

I don't know, but as I just did

Not knowing became obsolete

A magnificent feeling to deliver

My heart jumps and my blood shivers

Not that I'm cold

I'm as warm as Florida

LA winters

It's just the excitement of success

The thrill of doing what you love and giving your
best

Being in cahoots with yourself to accomplish a
common goal

Catching that feeling like a common cold

Then I caught her breath

Breaths later

Steps later

The journey isn't easy

But diamonds in the rough shine the same

Isn't that strange?

A tough route but I just go

I don't know everything

I just know

Dream On, Dreamers.

Breakdown

I just wanted to write. I didn't know what to write, but I felt inspired. The words just had to come out and I wanted to inspire someone. In life we never really know; but life still happens. We might as well do what we love and dream to do while we're here. I believe it is a lot less stressful. Sometimes things can be odd, abnormal, and unorthodox, but God works in mysterious ways, right? My faith is so strong that I am not worried at all about the unknown, and that's how we all must be, because we don't really know, we just believe. We all go to sleep with the notion that we will arise in the morning and do whatever we have planned for the next day, but you don't know for sure if that next day is promised. I live with that reality in all aspects. I know God blessed me with gifts and talents, and I believe I will achieve. I don't know

how, I just know.

Well Well Well

Well, well, well.

Guess I felt like writing again

Guess I felt that excitement again

A rush like nothing I've ever felt

I'm not just looking to make a woman's heart melt

I'm looking to inspire many

Move plenty

I have a story that could probably win an Emmy

Maybe an Oscar

Yeah!

I think that'll be proper

Never been a quitter or a stopper

I'm thinking giving up is awkward

Dabbled in procrastination

Definitely isn't my favorite

I have been a li'l lazy

But a hard worker

Ain't that crazy?

Dream chasing is amazing

Dream taking…

Now we're trailblazing

There's levels to this

I'm just escalating through

It's a passion.

Faith in God and love pulling me through

Far as I'm concerned I could never loose

If God is for me, who can be against me?

Point. Blank. Period. That's just the truth

Closer and closer

I can feel the heat

Escaping the past

Traveling through the present

Approaching my future

I can feel the heat

I'm running this race like a top-of-the-line athlete

It's all adding up

Making so much sense

Although much of my journey has been intense

Anything worth having has never really been on the

easy side of things

Flying high it's like I'm riding on wings

Perspective is big

Toughen up your mental

Mentality is instrumental

I just pray my words are influential

Inspiration to move forward

It's just what I'm into

Hey! Success!

I'm almost there

Girl, Ima get you

DREAM ON, DREAMERS!

Breakdown

Writing this was like creating, riding, and watching a roller coaster. I felt like writing, and it was a whirlwind. When I am inspired, I feel something different in my stomach. it's a rush, an experience, and I'm thankful for that feeling. My affinity for inspiring others has grown enormously over the years. I love hearing about friends, family, or even strangers being inspired by my God-given talent. As I continue to use that talent as a tool to accomplish goals in this journey we call life, I experience the good and the bad. Nevertheless, the throughways we call depression, down moments, human moments, hard times, or whatever your personal definition, are simply throughways or hallways to where we're destined to go. That's an amazing feeling. That's the message I want you to get when you read my words. I want you to get that feeling, but it all starts in the mind. If you really believe it, you can really achieve it.

As I Close My Eyes

As I close my eyes and what I see

What I envision some cannot be

But believe.

Believe in more than me

The Bible says as a man thinketh, so is he

Well, I'm a star

I'm a trendsetter

A risk-taker

A go-getter

I see more than simplicity

The level of difficulty is

A little tricky

I'm releasing stress

Well, I'm trying my best

But it's so much pain

That I can't find

It's no one chick that can be mine

There's too much life

No time for life

I try so hard

It hurts so bad

I'm so happy

But I feel so sad

My will is tough

My skin is, too

Built like a Ford

Prepared for the course

My daily journeys are prerequisites for life

Wired off emotion

My satisfaction is in success

Temporary happiness from sexual action

What is this orderly fashion?

What is this I'm facing for having a passion?

No matter how rocky or shaky

Nobody can make me

Not even maybe

Quitter is so far away from being associated with

me

Uncomfortable with the present and what's

happened lately

But with God I keep pressing

Won't nothing break me!

Words seem contradictive

But I'm only human

Searching for perfection

Struggling with progression

Fighting off regression

The stench of failure makes me nauseous

The thought makes my face squint

But the aroma of success

Ahhh…the thought of achievement

It's like the ultimate opposite

So far from bereavement

God wakes me up and the smell keeps me going

See, my heart is much bigger in size

Irregular growth

A dreamer's hope

It can be the bitter end

I still won't let go of the rope

Smiles and exclamations are at the next right

But how many more lefts before I can turn right?

It's okay I'll smile for now

Even during this fight

There's no way Ima give up

Not in this life…

DREAM ON, DREAMERS!

Breakdown

When writing this piece I closed my eyes and looked ahead. Ahead is where I looked because I am moving forward not backwards, not side to side, and I'm definitely not remaining stagnant. That is a mind-set, and we all must have the "look ahead" mind-set no matter what. Things are going to happen in life but no matter what, how, when, or where; until there's no breath in our bodies, we must continue on because life doesn't stop. How else do you expect to get where you are going? Breakups, deaths, disappointments, and failures are a part of the journey, but it's about the personal ability to keep moving forward and not become affixed with obstacles within the journey. No matter what happens, trust God, and stay focused.

Dream BIG

We're all kings and queens

With big dreams

Realistically we all want

Material things

And it starts with a dream

A vision.

The only way to get there

Is to oppose quittin'

Stopping is your only competition

How can you rise if you

Stop cooking?

How can you see it happen

If you stop looking?

Dream . . . Dream . . . Dream . . .

It's not wrong

If you want to

Write that song

Start that business

Action has no harm

You may find a passion

Something that lasts long

Like we say

Then you on

I just believe God didn't plant an empty seed

I'm sprouting.

It's something different in me

But we all have an X gene

Talents may be separation

But no one else is GOD

So no one else knows your destination

Incredible, ain't it?

You really can do what your heart desires

And let me tell you...Wow!

To be doing what you really love

Feels like my heart is on fire

God gave me these desires

You think he wouldn't provide water?

That's like an incomplete order

Moving forward, no torture

Challenging

I'm a soarer

Flying high with lost balloons

Abnormal as a full moon

Searching for more than the surface

Just makes more sense if you've noticed

I'm tired of hoping

Dreaming and motion

Big, not impossible

Giving up not probable

Holding on tight is just logical

The only way you know it's over is if you stop

The only way you know you made it is if not

Keep going. Dream big.

Find your spot.

Dreaming big is more than an interesting thought

Dream On, Dreamers.

Breakdown

This piece was inspired by my friend and great artist, Raheem Johnson. The artwork was something that I felt ran similar to my mind-set as a dreamer. There are no limits to my dreams because there are no limits to God and he created us all. We're all kings and queens, and there's nothing royalty can't have; but we must work for it. During that process things get challenging, but don't let up when the challenges come; push even harder. We want the reward but not the process it takes to get there. We're naturally meant to succeed, so a little work for a lot of success is actually logical. You have to believe it. I am not mediocre, and neither are you. Change your mind-set if you haven't already. Set your goals high and dream big. If you see big, that's what you will get. Even if it's not happening right now, keep fighting and faith your way to it.

Completion

The outpour of emotions

Tumbling out my mouth

Like an avalanche

Ignited by loud screams

That's how art escapes me

Similar to my dreams

Searching for a way out

An okay route

But what people don't know

Is I've began a loud roar

A guaranteed stretch of my vocal cords

That even in the circle of life

Species would be amazed by my volumes

Monsoons and full moons

Are what I expect

How could I settle for less?

Wouldn't you? No? Don't you want the best?

I mean, women want diamonds

Men want cars

Everybody wants to be a star, but few truly want to

work hard

Stating the obvious and some probably hoped for an

incomplete sentence

Well, that's not how you get in that acute

percentage

My heart growls with excitement

When releasing

I guess I'm a special species

But aren't we all?

Aren't we all special and incredible?

Unique and mixed with our own personal

characteristics

Dreams and pains

Covered in our own stains

Yet afraid of the rain

My message to the world is go for it all

Leave nothing untapped

No gifts unwrapped

Negativity is a trap

A mental lapse falling short of faith

Just trust GOD!

Hold on to mercy and grace

Everything you've ever wanted

Open your eyes

It's directly in your face

Just start.

No time for perfect planning

Attack like Runyon Canyon

I can imagine the top is similar to achieving your
goals

Nothing like poker for me because I will never fold

No quitting; I will compete

These talents

The arts

Goals

And my dreams

I will complete

DREAM ON, DREAMERS!

Breakdown

This piece was written at the top of Runyon
Canyon in Los Angeles, California. It was a day I
just wanted to write but I had the urge to write at the
top of the mountain, symbolizing completion. It is

really a journey to the top and it isn't easy. I sweated a lot, I was tired, I had to ration my water, it hurt; but the feeling at the top after the journey was amazing. This is just like life. We are constantly on journeys, and we can't procrastinate or hesitate. We have to get to it, start somewhere. That is how you reach completion. How do you know you made it if you don't start, and how do you know you didn't if you stop?

I Came Too Far

I came too far to hang it all up

It's been too hard

To hang it all up...now that,

That would be funny

I'm writing my life book

How to Dream for Dummies

I moved to where it's always sunny

Where you have to fight with every inch of your

being

Where the beginning can be the ending

And winning is upon me

Where when the holidays come people say they

haven't seen their family in years

When I think of my family I'm damn near in tears

See, I have some family that's no longer here

So the ones that are

Will never go to the rear

I not only do this for myself

But for my family and friends

And my future family's wealth

I'm too close, like a crowded train at the end of a

shift

My mind is crowded with positive mist

Negativity is always dismissed

And will never be missed

I never work those muscles

I'm unfit to fit the quit list

God ain't broke so you can't fix this

I'm a misfit

I go against the grain like a bad haircut

Ask my momma

She knows what's up

I guess I just don't give a WHAT

See, all I know is how to keep pushing

Even when I fall and there's no cushion

I pick myself up and dust myself off

I look up and say thank you for favor

It'll never be easy

It even took six days for the Creator

Let me tell you what's in my nature

This race is a journey and I go hard like a track star

Like a bully, I won't back off

I'm constantly saved by the bell

Guess you can't take Zack off

My glass is half-full always

Smile on my face

Flowing through hallways

Even on saw days

That day killed me

Softly like Lauryn Hill

It's a miseducation so I'm going still

But I won't become stagnant

I'm just fighting patiently

Taking action

Our biggest critics live in the mirror

No satisfaction

All you magicians sitting

Waiting for magic

Until things get drastic

Then you become dramatic

I've been a victim

I'm a creature of habit

Nipped that in the bud when I changed my habit

I'm not having it.

I won't die without taking a stab at it

As a matter of fact

I'm grabbing it

No, sir; no, ma'am

Can't hang it up

Just know, dreamers, what you're doing it for

This journey is dangerous

Dream On, Dreamers.

Breakdown

This piece was initially written as a response to two of my close friends, Kev and Kado. It was my third year in LA, and I was going home to Virginia for a couple months. They told me I would not come back, it was "over." They had seen this before with a number of people. I knew that I would not be placed in that category. I had been through too much and come too far to give up. Every line in this poem is real to me. To hang it all up would be letting all of the prior experiences be for nothing, all the hard work for nothing, all the miracle watching for nothing, and I knew it was for something. You have to know that if you're alive, it's for a reason. Everything you have been through is just preparation for things to come; greatness comes with a price. Just stay the course and trust God on the journey; we've all come too far to hang it all up!

3-Piece No. 1

The intermingling design

How she and success intertwine

A male at his best

That would be mighty fine

But what is his best?

Does effort get straddled in ideologies?

Are nicks and bruises not a part of that realm of

biology

Or am I being microscopic

Everyone speaks of imperfection not being a

problem

But we're all guilty of it being the hot topic

The specifics we request

How could shallow be a description that anyone
suggests

Along with our pursued happiness?

It's the no stress that we're most happy with

So difficult to just live in this diverse world

Some say it's okay to pour out pain

Some have a much further extreme

Look on you with disdain

It's strange.

Often unsettled by thoughts racing and rambling
through my head

Disrupted by real life emotion

That leaves me cooped up instead

Left on a battlefield full of known enemies

It's like a lifelong penitentiary

And freedom is what we seek

But the quest is sometimes accompanied by hurt

It's probably the toughest

Because when you feel you've finally overcome a

pain

That sliced your life like half a pie

It's like vengeance appears and removes an eye

But faith has to reappear somehow

Because "vengeance is mine," sayeth the Lord

It can't be contradictory

But it is specifically and dynamically written for

you

BOO!

Scared much?

Maybe a little

Finding out pain comes with life sucks

Finding out Pain comes with Life sucks

FINDING OUT PAIN COMES WITH LIFE

SUCKS!

Over and over again

But it's about getting back up

Showing someone else that has fallen

That for your dream you're all in

Mustering the strength to succeed when you're tired

of falling down

An awful sound

When the base to love and a successful career are

polar opposites to near and here

When it seems every time you're almost in front

It's like someone places you in a deep slumber and

you arise in the rear

How is it that you carry on?

Jesus himself looked death in the eye and defeated

it for us all

There's no way I'll let pain be responsible for my

fall

DREAM ON, DREAMERS!

Breakdown

Writing this piece, I had no clue it would be the beginning to a 3-piece set, literally. I call this one the right cross. I want to convey that success and love run parallel, and eventually intertwine from the start. We have no control of what happens on the journey, but we have control of our mind-set. I believe that we marry into our destiny, so when I experienced my first heartbreak and my career wasn't where I wanted it to be, I was slightly distraught. I was very analytical at that point and at times an over-thinker. Sometimes pain affects us in ways we think never possible, but we have to keep the mentality that not even the hurt can deter us from reaching and achieving goals. You have to be able to get back up if you fall because you will probably fall again. Preparation is huge when it comes to moving forward in anything, especially life. If you have fallen before, although it may be a different stumbling block, you will already have learned how to dust off, get up, and keep moving. That's just the beginning, because once you start moving again, you still have to develop the gumption and build on the trust in God to keep moving.

3-Piece No. 2

Utterly disgusted with my physical disposition

Driving me to be emotionless

Cold as a hollow soul

How awkward, seeing that I'm always preaching

tomorrow's glow

I feel I'm slowly unraveling

Simultaneously still battling

It's so weird

Almost fear

What's the cure?

I thought love

But she's an illusion

Spent so much time blues'n

But when you look back at all the cruisin'

What goes around comes around

At some point I had to sit down

I feel I'm not fit to frown

So when I am down it's like my world is upside

down

Inside out and turned around

If I could walk away from my life I would...

I can't.

That's what hurts the most

It's surely a problem; I can barely handle jokes

Yo necesito mi padre

But he passed away

So what can I say?

But move on to the next day

But who can I truly talk with?

No judging, just pouring out my heart with

As positive as I am I feel

I sometimes can't escape darkness

I could use the smile of sunshine

Just a tease is one time

Although a fun time

I like forever mine

My mind wanders so many places

I've seen so many faces

Habitual

I know, crazy!

Anytime I look to discontinue

I send a personal missile

The entire circumference of my life

A cloud of failure looms above

Some sunrays; but I still see night

GOD where is the LIGHT!?

I have to make better decisions and I take full

accountability

But, man, something ain't right

Things I go through

Although make me tougher

Man, it's tough to go through

Pain I shoulder

So glad I don't own a holster

I'm only getting older

Although warmer, it seems I'm only getting colder

But what is outside perspective?

Possibly a reflection of my direction

Or maybe a misdirection

Hear me through my vocal inflection

Before I'm dead and gone

I'll be more than well respected

Not because of me, but because GOD is my director

DREAM ON, DREAMERS!

Breakdown

This is the left hook. It comes after awakening with the idea and understanding that pain comes with life, but it doesn't have to control your life or your mentality. We must continue on regardless if we want to be successful, but continuing on is easier said than done. I'm a very optimistic and faithful person, but there are times where I am literally disgusted with where I am in life and how I am handling that current position, although I know ultimately it is just a temporary location...remember, you won't be there forever. You can feel like it's the end or at least close to it; I know I did. But even when it seems like you are furthest away from where you are headed, something happens to let you know you are right where you are supposed to be. We are all headed

71

where we're supposed to go, but how will our journeys be handled, and will we detour ourselves with temporary situations that are negative and not positive enhancers?

My first heartbreak coupled with slow progress had me reeling for my deceased father, pitifully believing the worst of myself, and tossing thoughts to and fro that couldn't help me if I paid them heed. See, you get to a point where you understand that pain has to happen; there have to be downs for there to be ups. But you still have to go through those downs. We still have to experience that pain. It is another level to push through those periods of life. No matter what, you must believe that God has it all under control, and whatever your purpose is on this earth, it will be served. Leave it all in his hands—even amongst the chaos, he's an awesome director.

3-Piece No. 3

As a tear rests upon my face and the emotions

appear through my pen

I just give what I can

As a person

As a man.

It's said a drunk mind brings sober thoughts

So what about the truth that spews out

When not intoxicated people find it hard to believe?

Inebriated, and people wear their hearts on their

sleeves

Not saying that is a problem

But it does pose a question

I know for me it begins a new lesson

Mistakes Can Ruin Your Life Part 1

I now ponder where I started from

This just has to be a replica of the initiation

I've long been a member of the mistaken

I once thought I was located at a lifelong safe haven

Never alluded the raven

Must've been mistaken

A friend once said you found out you're human…

What a confirmation!

Pain sucks as understanding

The sickness forces you to be a patient

But all my life

I'm tired of being patient

Where is my bliss?

My pure happiness

Struggle—leave me be

Broken hearts

Caused by me

And brought to me

Struggle—leave me be!

In my ideal world

I illustrate as a Picasso

Or Michelangelo

Blow sounds as a Louis Armstrong

And move to tunes like a Gregory Hines

Success and happiness

In Jesus' name

Is mine

DREAM ON, DREAMERS!

Breakdown

This is the knockout punch. This is where you

conclude the combination. The 3-piece became "3-

Piece" because I wrote them back to back to back

and they packed such a powerful punch. As I

concluded this last one and read them all I knew they were a combination of powerful words to help and inspire. I thank God for the words he gives me. I was going through some awful pain at this time, and I literally cried as I wrote this last piece. All I know is to give all I can, and I feel I do that in all aspects, especially ones that matter to me most.

We get to a place where we run the list of things that are wrong and contribute to our current funk or stupor through our heads over and over again. Then you have to combine getting back up and getting moving again with the power punch, the belief that no matter what, success and happiness is "MINE" in Jesus' name. That's when you understand who you truly are and how amazing you are. We were created in greatness, and our lives are just journeys back to greatness, just an evolution to

77

a new level of greatness. Once you unlock that superpower in yourself, you are unstoppable. It doesn't mean that sometimes things won't be challenging, and you'll experience what I call "human moments," but you will have a different approach and handle it a little better each time. Nothing can stop us! We have God, and that's a real knockout punch.

Mother's Day Every Day

Once upon a time, a smart, young girl from a small

town in Florida grew into a woman.

I mean, I don't know everything, but I know she

was on it.

Some say she was tarnished

I say after child she grew strongest

Never backing down

Facing every opponent

My momma…

Who I first learned to be strong with

And you have strong wit

Words…even yelling, like a songstress

From one to seven you've been the best mom with

T's and L's doing, and have done very well

So much adversity and you never falter

A God-fearing woman leaving it all at the altar

Thank you from 0 to 29

I thank God you're mine

Mother

Momma

Teacher

Friend

So many things!

You and Daddy made it comfortable to dream

Like I can accomplish anything

I mean

You had me as a teen

You turned out to be a queen

What a lot of young women dream to be

Everything ain't what it seems to be

But God's blessing nevertheless

You are a blessing, the best!

The best momma a son or daughter could have

It's been tough but you taught me how to last

Your big ol' house is coming soon like a

Hollywood blockbuster

The big payoff; and it won't be lackluster

More like when they first created ketchup and

mustard

Yes, ma'am, it's almost your turn!

Your turn to sit down and rest your nerves a little

bit

Get ready because it's coming quick

I love you so much

My appreciation is iron-tough

A fairytale mother accomplishing so many things

I guess it is what it seems

Once upon a time my mother started as a teen

A long, yellow brick road; but you get what you
need

Now look at you…

Momma, you doing your thing

I'm so proud of you

My first queen.

Breakdown

My mother means the world to me. I
originally wrote this for Mother's Day, and when I
was piecing this book together I had to include it as
a dedication to the woman who birthed me. *What is
my first book without my momma?* were my
thoughts. She's never given up on me and has
always been there for me. Alexis Celeste Carter,
mother of seven, friend, confidant, sister, daughter,
leader, entrepreneur, and more; I love you dearly,

and thank you so much. To me, it's Mother's Day every day because you never cease at being the greatest mother I know. Happy Mother's Day!

Made in the USA
Columbia, SC
12 June 2022